Alfred E. Smith, former governor of New York, headed the Empire State Building Corporation.

Cornerstones of Freedom

The Story of

THE EMPIRE STATE BUILDING

By Patrick Clinton

CHILDRENS PRESS ®

CHICAGO

The Waldorf-
Astoria Hotel on
the corner of Fifth
Avenue and 34th
Street was built in
1892.

Library of Congress Cataloging-in-Publication Data

Clinton, Patrick.

The story of the Empire State Building.
(Cornerstones of freedom)
Summary: Describes the planning and building of what
was once the world's tallest building and examines how
it fit into the growth of New York City.
1.   Empire State Building (New York, N.Y.) — Juvenile
literature. 2.   New York (N.Y.) — Buildings, structures,
etc. — Juvenile literature. [1.   Empire State Building
(New York, N.Y.) 2.   New York (N.Y.) — Buildings,
structures, etc. 3. Buildings] I. Title. II. Series.
F128.8.E46C56   1987   974.7'1'   87-25687
ISBN 0-516-04730-2

Childrens Press®, Chicago
Copyright ©1987 by Regensteiner Publishing Enterprises, Inc.
All rights reserved. Published simultaneously in Canada.
Printed in the United States of America.
1 2 3 4 5 6 7 8 9 10 R 96 95 94 93 92 91 90 89 88 87

John J. Raskob

One day in 1929, John Jacob Raskob walked through the streets of New York City. Raskob had been born poor, but now he was rich and powerful. He had worked his way up through the DuPont Chemical Company and helped found General Motors, one of America's biggest and most successful businesses. Today, though, he had a new project in mind.

Raskob led his companion to the corner of Fifth Avenue and 34th Street. He pointed to the building on the corner, the Waldorf-Astoria Hotel. The hotel was a New York City landmark. For years, it was the place where the wealthy stayed when they visited the city, where tycoons and visiting royalty dined and held splendid parties. Now it was closed.

"You see that site over there?" Raskob asked. "We're going to build the biggest and the highest building in the entire world over there."

A few months later, an architect named William Frederick Lamb sat at his drawing board working on Raskob's dream. It wasn't easy. Not only did Lamb and his partners have to design the world's tallest building, they had to make sure that it was ready to open on May 1, 1931—just eighteen months away. No one had ever built a building that tall that fast.

There were many decisions to make: What shape should the offices be? Where should the elevators and plumbing go? How tall a building could they afford to build with the money Raskob and his partners had to spend? What should the building look like?

Lamb picked up a big pencil and set it on end on his drawing board. That was the look he wanted—slim and sleek, like an arrow pointing into the sky. He started sketching. Lamb's first plan for the new building wasn't quite right. Neither was the second nor the third. He changed the shape of the floors, the top of the tower, the look and feel of the outside of the building. Finally he had it. The Empire State Building.

A five-story base would fill the lot. The entrance would be four stories high, the lobby, three. On top of this base a slim, tapering tower would rise eighty-six floors. The windows were set flush with the out-

Architect William F. Lamb
(inset) and the nearly
completed Empire State
Building

The exterior of the Empire State Building is made of Indiana limestone and granite.

side walls and separated by shining metal strips. This made the building look even taller. Lamb had designed his sleek "pencil."

On the corner of Fifth Avenue and 34th Street, workmen tore down the old Waldorf-Astoria. They hauled the rubble out to sea and started to work on the new tower. The foundations went in. Then a mighty steel frame shot into the air faster than anyone had ever seen before—a floor a week, week in and week out. Trucks lined up at the construction site, delivering steel, bricks, cable, marble, concrete.

On May 1, 1931, the world's tallest building was ready. Alfred E. Smith, the former governor of New York and the head of the Empire State Building

Corporation, was the host of an official celebration. Thousands of people crowded the sidewalks as Smith's granddaughter and grandson, Mary and Arthur, cut a ribbon to open the building. (Actually, the ribbon wouldn't cut, and Smith finally had to rip it out of the way.) At 11:30 A.M., in Washington, D.C., President Herbert Hoover pushed a button that turned on the lights in the building.

Then there was a luncheon for three hundred fifty guests on the eighty-sixth floor. "I'd like you to remember that you are eating higher up in the air

In the lobby of the building, guests gather for its official opening. The lobby was made of marble imported from Italy, France, Belgium, and Germany.

New York building superintendent, Frederick C. Kuehnle, hands Al Smith a certificate of occupancy during the dedication ceremonies.

than any human being has ever eaten," Smith said. "There may have been loftier meals on mountaintops or in airplanes, but not in buildings. This is the world's record." There were speeches. "Probably no building in the history of the world has brought about such universal interest in its progress," Smith said. "The Empire State Building stands today as the greatest monument to ingenuity, to skill, to brain power, to muscle power, the tallest thing in the world today produced by the hand of man."

But the real star was the view. (On a clear day you can see eighty miles from the Empire State Building, into New Jersey, Pennsylvania, Connecticut, and Massachusetts, as well as New York.) All day long visitors poured through the observatory to see a sight few of them had seen before: New York City spread out below them. The steamships on the Hudson and East rivers looked like tugboats. Fifth Avenue and Broadway were slender ribbons between rows of buildings that looked strange and new when seen from above.

The architect, William Lamb, wasn't there; he had set sail for Europe. Still, he sent a telegram from his ship, and Al Smith read it at the opening: "One day out and I can still see the building."

New York City's skyline had a new crown, the Empire State Building.

Today the island of Manhattan—which contains the center of New York City—is almost completely covered with buildings and streets. It looks manmade, and it is easy to forget that it was ever anything but a city.

Two hundred years ago, though, most of Manhattan was farmland. New York City thrived on the southern part of the island, but the rest was green and crisscrossed with creeks. When John Thompson bought the land where the Empire State Building stands today, it had never even been plowed. Thompson was the first to build there; his house and barn probably stood not far from where passengers board the Empire State Building's express elevator.

Empire State Building (top center)

John Jacob Astor (left). The lobby of the
Waldorf-Astoria Hotel (above right) as it looked
shortly after it was built.

Gradually Thompson's farm became part of the city—a very fashionable part. In 1859, John Jacob Astor built one of New York's richest and most famous houses on the spot. A few years later, his brother William Backhouse Astor built *his* house nearby. New York's very richest inhabitants lived in the surrounding neighborhood. The mansions stood a little more than thirty years; then came the Waldorf-Astoria, and roughly forty years later, the Empire State Building.

Why did the neighborhood change? It was partly because of land prices. Thompson paid only two thousand six hundred dollars for his land in 1799. But as the city grew, land became more and more valuable. Thompson's twenty acres sold for ten thousand dollars in 1827, and for twice that much just two years later. When Raskob and his partners bought just two acres of the land, about one hundred years later, they paid sixteen million dollars! The land was too valuable to be a farm or a house, or even a hotel.

Why was it worth so much?

The most important reason is that New York City grew. It had long been one of America's most important cities, but by the beginning of the twentieth century, it was by far the largest city and the most important port in North America. It was the second largest city in the world. Only London, England, had a larger population.

When John Thompson bought his farm in 1799, there were about 33,000 people in New York City. By 1861 there were 500,000, and soon after the Civil War there were a million. At the turn of the century, the island of Manhattan was bursting at the seams. The city had almost three and one-half million people. All of them needed places to live and work. To meet their needs, the city extended its boundaries across the Hudson and East rivers and into the surrounding countryside.

Roughly the same thing happened in all of America's big cities: The cities grew and houses

replaced farms at the edges of the city, where land was inexpensive. Then, as land prices went up, businesses moved in and people moved farther away. What used to be the edge of the city became a part of the center. For example, the Thompson farm was several miles from New York City when it was first built; but the Empire State Building, on the same piece of property, stands near the center of New York City today.

Remember, in the nineteenth and early twentieth centuries, there were no cars, no buses or subways, no freeways, no telephones. The cities couldn't afford to spread out. Businesses needed to be close together, and a central location was important.

So cities didn't just grow out, they grew up.

Horse-drawn carriages lined up at the entrance to the Waldorf-Astoria, 1898.

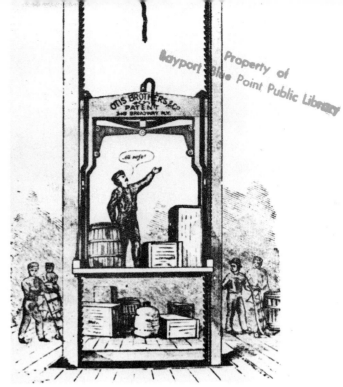

Early passenger elevator (above) and freight
elevator (right), patented by the Otis
brothers.

It wasn't easy. Tall buildings had two great problems to solve. First, most people were not willing to
walk up and down the stairs in a building taller than
five stories. Although various types of elevators had
been around for centuries, they had had the same
things wrong with them — they were too slow and
too dangerous. The average elevator was a box at
the end of a rope — and if the rope broke, the box fell.
So freight rode in elevators, and people, for the most
part, didn't.

This problem was solved in the 1850s when Elisha
Otis invented a safety elevator. It was still a box and
a rope, but the box also rode along a metal rail,
something like a train track. And if the rope broke

...well, Otis, at public events, used to demonstrate what would happen. He'd set up a tall, open elevator, ride it to the top, and then have someone cut the rope. As the rope went slack and the car began to fall, a spring device would grab the rail and stop the car. "All safe, gentlemen," Otis would call to the crowd below.

Within a few years, passenger elevators were becoming common, and buildings started to get taller — instead of five stories, they started reaching ten, fifteen, even twenty stories into the air.

But before buildings could get taller, something else would have to change — the way they were built.

Until the eve of the twentieth century, buildings were always made the same way: the walls held up the weight of the structure. That's a fine way to build if you want only a five- or six-story building. But if you get much taller, the walls have to be extremely thick. For example, the Monadnock Building, built in 1891 in Chicago, was the tallest building ever built with "load-bearing" walls. It was sixteen stories tall, and its walls on the first floor were fifteen feet thick.

In 1885, in Chicago, an architect named William LeBaron Jenney tried something different. He built a ten-story building supported by a skeleton of iron and steel. The walls didn't have to hold up the building. The roof, the floors, and even the walls themselves were supported by the skeleton, the way the human skeleton supports the weight of the body. The walls were just a skin to keep out the elements. As a result, they could be thinner, lighter, and easier to design and build.

Because iron was soft, heavy, and easily damaged by fire, architects began building with steel beams. Steel is much better for building than iron—stronger, harder, and lighter. New York City's first all-steel framed building was the twenty-six story World Building, completed in 1890.

View of City Hall and Newspaper Row, 1899, with the World Building (center left)

With safe elevators and steel frame construction, there seemed almost no limit to how high a building could go. Soon, in New York City, the race for the sky was on. In 1909, Metropolitan Life Insurance Company built a 700-foot-tall building. In 1913, the Woolworth Building went 792 feet into the air. By 1930, New York City had the world's tallest building: the Chrysler Building, 1,046 feet tall—62 feet taller than the Eiffel Tower.

And the Empire State Building was on the way.

An architect doesn't get to make all the decisions about a building. Many of them are made for him, by the client, by the nature of the building he's designing, and even by the city where it's going to be built.

The Metropolitan Life Insurance Company (below) and the Woolworth Building (right)

The Chrysler Building (above)
and the Eiffel Tower (right) in
Paris, France

William Lamb's clients made simple demands on him: They gave him a budget and a deadline; said the walls should be limestone and that offices should measure 26 feet from hallway to window. Then they told Lamb to give them the tallest building their money would buy.

The city's rules were more complicated. The city didn't want tall buildings to block out the sunlight, so there were laws on how large a building could be. You could build on your whole property, but only up to a certain height. You could build as tall as you wanted only on about a quarter of your property. Lamb studied the laws. They gave him a set of boundaries he couldn't ignore in designing the Empire State Building.

What's the most important floor when you're designing a tall building? The ground floor? "There are buildings in which the ground floor plan has been permitted to control the balance of the building," William Lamb once said. "The result is not often fortunate and is frequently disastrous." Lamb thought it was best to start designing with one of the office floors. He arranged the office space around a "core" that contained elevators, stairwells, plumbing, and so forth. Once he had designed a typical office floor, it was easy to draw plans for the tower above and the ground floors below.

Lamb didn't just design the building, however. He had to plan how it would be built quickly.

Remember, Raskob and his partners weren't building the Empire State Building for themselves to use. It was an investment. It's expensive to build a big building. As soon as you buy land, you have to pay taxes on it. As soon as you borrow money, you have to start paying it back—with interest. Raskob and his partners needed to get rent from their tenants as soon as they could. And that meant they needed the building as soon as they could get it.

And so the architects and the construction company invented a new, faster way of building. They treated the Empire State Building like an assembly line stood on end. Different workers performed different tasks on each floor. When their work was done they moved on to the next floor.

Builders used 60,000 tons of steel in the Empire State Building (enough to build two railroad tracks from New York to Baltimore), 60 miles of water pipe, and 3,500 miles of telephone and telegraph wire.

As soon as the final plans were drawn for the ground floors, the orders went out to the steel mills for the materials needed. And the architects went back to work on the drawings for the next floor. As soon as the steel was delivered, the construction crews started assembling it, and the mills started to work on the orders for the next floor. Work overlapped: the drawings for the eightieth floor weren't completed until about the time the steel frame of the ground floor was being built. Electricians and plasterers worked on the lower floors, while high above them, workers put together the steel frame, and the roof was still a drawing in the architect's office. Before the building was finished a "hat" had been added to the design—a mooring mast for airships was built that reached to the 102nd floor.

Work was done in factories throughout the world. Steel beams were cut to precise lengths; parts were shaped to exact drawings—so that workers on the bustling building site wouldn't have to stop and make adjustments. Like workers in an auto factory, they would just assemble the same parts over and over again, floor by floor.

Day in, day out, truckloads of supplies arrived, all according to a minute-by-minute schedule. On each floor, a little railroad carried supplies to the place they were needed. There was no waiting.

An electrician completes construction of the television antenna atop the Empire State Building.

Work was amazingly fast. The whole fifty-seven-thousand-ton steel structure took twenty-five weeks to build. The limestone walls went up at roughly a story per day, and there were ten days in which workmen managed to finish fourteen. All in all, the Empire State Building took about a year to build—which in those days, was as long as it took to build one about half its size.

There was a cost for the extra speed. When the Chrysler Building was built, only one worker was killed in an accident. Fourteen men were killed working on the Empire State Building.

After the great rush to get the Empire State Building ready for its tenants, John Jacob Raskob must have been disappointed. Only about a quarter of the offices were rented. Indeed, it wasn't until many years later that even half of the building was rented. Raskob had chosen a good location, and he'd built a wonderful building, but had chosen a bad time to do it. The stock market crashed in 1929, just about the time the Waldorf-Astoria Hotel was torn down, and by the time the Empire State Building was opened in 1931, the country was deep in the Great Depression.

Although the building wasn't a financial success at first, the people still loved it. Millions visited the observation deck, or bought models of the building. The Empire State Building became a symbol of New

York City, and of America, rather like the Statue of Liberty. At a time when business was having a hard time, it was a reminder of what business could do. At a time when dreams seemed impossible to achieve, it was a dream that came true in steel and stone.

The building appeared in more than 150 movies. The most famous, of course, was the original *King Kong*, made in 1933. In the film, the giant ape climbs to the top of the Empire State Building to fight his final battle. The building seems to stand for civilization and progress and technology—all the things King Kong is not.

Fire caused by a plane crash (right) quickly spread through the top floors of the Empire State Building. After the fire was put out, reporters scurried to the 28th floor (left) to cover the story.

No giant ape ever climbed the Empire State Building, but the building did have one disaster that might have come out of a movie. One foggy Saturday morning in 1945, a bomber got lost on its way to Newark, New Jersey. It crashed into the Empire State Building between the seventy-eighth and seventy-ninth floors. The wings were torn off, and the plane ripped a hole in the side of the building eighteen feet wide and twenty feet high. One engine fell down an elevator shaft, and the other went through the building, made a hole in the opposite wall, and landed on the roof of a nearby building.

The plane's fuel exploded, and flames shot up to the observatory on the eighty-sixth floor. Flaming gasoline ran down stairways and out into the hallways down to the seventy-fifth floor. It was the world's highest fire, but luckily it took only about forty minutes to put out. The crash caused half a million dollars worth of damage, and thirteen people were killed—including the three in the plane.

The Empire State Building never was the home of large corporations, as Raskob expected. Instead, over the years, it has attracted a variety of smaller businesses. (Some of them had problems being in the world's tallest building. The building bends slightly when the wind is strong. One jeweler used to complain that he couldn't weigh diamonds when the wind was blowing. The movement of the building threw his scales off.) Today, about half of the building is rented by dealers in men's clothing and men's and women's shoes.

The airship mast at the top of the Empire State Building was seldom used. The great airships were nearly as long as the Empire State Building is tall, and it was too difficult to keep them from swaying in the wind. There were a few experiments (one time, a blimp delivered newspapers to the building), but then the idea was abandoned.

The World Trade Center (left) and the Sears Tower in Chicago (right)

Today the Empire State Building is no longer the world's tallest. The Sears Tower in Chicago is 110 stories and 1,454 feet tall. The twin towers of the World Trade Center in New York are each 110 stories—1,350 feet high—and one of them has a TV antenna that reaches 1,601 feet. For a while the architectural firm of Shreve, Lamb, and Harmon worked on plans to add on to the Empire State Building and make it once again the world's tallest—113 stories and 1,494 feet high. Eventually they gave up.

In 1981, the building quietly turned fifty years old. Its life goes on. Each day, sixteen thousand people go to work there. Another thirty-five thousand come each day to visit and do business. Each year about two million people visit the observatories on the 86th and 102nd floors to enjoy the famous view. They all know the Empire State Building is no longer the world's tallest, but somehow it doesn't matter. There are plenty of tall buildings in the world, but the Empire State Building has always managed to be something more.

Al Waquie of Jemez, New Mexico, climbed the 1,575 steps of the Empire State Building to win the Eighth Annual Empire State Building Run-Up.

About the Author

Pat Clinton has his master's degree from Northwestern University. He was the managing editor of the *Reader* for eight years and is currently a senior editor at *Chicago* magazine. He lives in Chicago with his wife, Susan, and their two sons.